Snap books™

Crafts

Fingernail Art

Dazzling Fingers and Terrific Toes

by Thiranut Boonyadhistarn

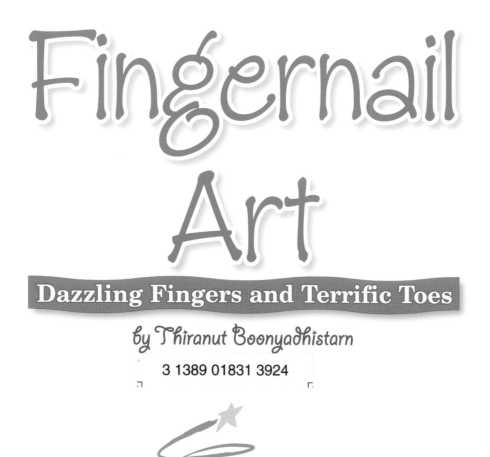

Capstone press®

Mankato, Minnesota

Snap Books are published by Capstone Press,
151 Good Counsel Drive, P.O. Box 669, Mankato, Minnesota 56002.
www.capstonepress.com

Library of Congress Cataloging-in-Publication Data
Boonyadhistarn, Thiranut.
    Fingernail art : dazzling fingers and terrific toes / by Thiranut
Boonyadhistarn.
        p. cm.—(Snap books. Crafts)
    Includes bibliographical references and index.
    ISBN-13: 978-0-7368-6474-9 (hardcover)
    ISBN-10: 0-7368-6474-1 (hardcover)
    1. Nail art (Manicuring)—Juvenile literature. I. Title. II. Series.
TT958.3.B66 2007
646.7'27—dc22   2006004084

Summary: A do-it-yourself crafts book for children and pre-teens
    on fingernail art.

Editor: Megan Schoeneberger
Designer: Bobbi J. Wyss
Production Artist: Renée T. Doyle
Photo Researcher: Kelly Garvin

Photo Credits:
Aubrey Whitten, 32; Capstone Press/TJ Thoraldson Digital Photography, cover (objects and hand), 5, 6, 7, 9, 10 (all), 11 (all),
12, 13 (both), 15, 16, 17, 19, 20 (all), 21, 22, 23, 25, 26 (all), 27; Corbis/Michelle Garrett, 28 (left); Photodisc/Barbara Penoyar,
cover (girl); Shutterstock/Bart Tan, 28 (right); Shutterstock/Sergey Tokarev aka Lahtak, 29 (left)

Capstone Press wishes to thank nail artist Janelle Gens for her help in preparing this book.

1 2 3 4 5 6 11 10 09 08 07 06

6/07

Go Metric!

It's easy to change measurements to metric! Just use this chart.

To change	into	multiply by
inches	centimeters	2.54
inches	millimeters	25.4
feet	meters	.305
yards	meters	.914
ounces (liquid)	milliliters	29.57
ounces (liquid)	liters	.029
cups (liquid)	liters	.237
pints	liters	.473
quarts	liters	.946
gallons	liters	3.78
ounces (dry)	grams	28.35
pounds	grams	453.59

Table of Contents

CHAPTER 1

No More Plain Polish

What do your nails say about you?

If your nails are plain now, they'll say a lot more once you give nail art a try. You can paint your nails any color of the rainbow. Jazz them up with **rhinestones**, glitter, and stickers galore. Whether your nails are long or short, the projects in this book will make them stand out in a crowd.

Get Your Gear

In addition to the polishes of your choice, here's a list of some other basics you'll need to get started:

buffers—small sponges covered with sandpaper for buffing your nails

clear nail polish—polish without any color, often used as an **adhesive**, **sealant**, and top coat

emery boards—boards used to file and shape your nails; stay away from metal nail files. They can actually damage your nails.

nailbrush—a small brush for cleaning fingernails; use the softest one you can find.

nail clippers—a tool for cutting fingernails and toenails

nail polish remover—a liquid used to take off nail polish

rubbing alcohol—a liquid that cleans oil from your nails to help keep polish from chipping

toe separators—foam sponges that fit between your toes to keep them apart while you paint your toenails

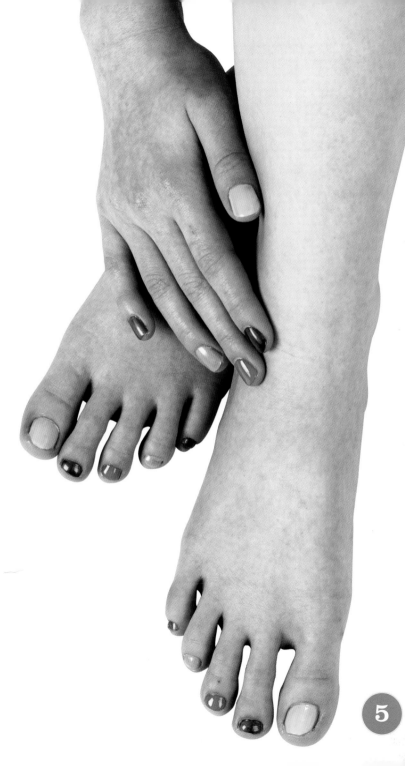

CHAPTER 2

Ready, set, Prep

Pamper your nails before you polish!

Before you begin, give your hands or feet the royal treatment with a **manicure** or **pedicure**. Getting rid of dirt and oils will help your nail art stay fresh and chip-free longer.

Here's what you need

* nail clippers
* emery board
* nail buffer
* mild soap
* large bowl or basin filled with warm, soapy water
* nailbrush
* manicure stick
* hand towel
* tissues
* rubbing alcohol

Here's what you do

1. Clip and trim your nails.

2. File your nails. Always file in one direction, never back and forth.

3. Buff the surface of your nails with a fine buffer. Buffing will help keep your polish from chipping.

4. Soak your nails in warm, sudsy water for 5 minutes.

5. Scrub your nails with a soft brush. Remove any stubborn dirt from under your nails with a manicure stick.

6. Rinse and dry your hands or feet and nails.

7. Moisten a tissue with rubbing alcohol and use it to clean any traces of oil from your nails.

CHAPTER 3

Lovely Little Polka Dots

Who doesn't love polka dots?

Polka dots never go out of style. Play around with different colors, dot sizes, and patterns. Try painting the dots straight across, in zigzags, or just randomly. The colorful combinations go on and on!

Here's what you need

* 1 color nail polish for base coat and 1 or more colors nail polish for polka dots (**opaque** colors work best)
* toothpicks
* clear nail polish

Blow It Dry

Always make sure the first coat of polish is dry to the touch before you apply the next coat. You can speed it up with a hair dryer set to low heat. After about 5 minutes, test your nails. If they're still sticky to the touch, blow-dry for another 5 minutes.

Here's what you do

1 Apply a base coat and let it dry. If needed, add a second coat. Make sure it's dry before you start the next step.

2 For the dots, dip the end of a toothpick into the polish color you want and dot the color on top of the base coat.

3 Repeat step 2 in whatever pattern you like.

4 After the dots dry, apply a clear coat over your nails.

Punch It

Having trouble with the dots? There's another way. Get yourself a hole punch that punches little tiny dots. Then grab some medium-weight paper or even a piece of craft foil. Now punch away!

Applying the dots is easy. Paint your base color and let it dry completely. Then add a coat of clear polish. This time, don't wait for it to dry. Dip the end of a toothpick into the bottle of clear polish. Use it to pick up a dot and place it on your nail. When you're finished, wait 10 to 15 minutes, and then apply two clear coats over the dots.

Rolling the Dice
Look like Lady Luck with this winning design. Apply two coats of base color. Then use a contrasting color to add the dots to look like dice.

CHAPTER 4

Starry, Starry Night

Twinkle, twinkle, you're the star.

Want a **glamorous** look for your nails that will dazzle and shine? You'll really look like a star with these sparkling nails. This dreamy design will turn heads on any occasion, day or night.

Here's what you need

* blue shimmer nail polish
* silver glitter polish
* toothpick
* small star confetti or decals in silver or light blue
* clear nail polish

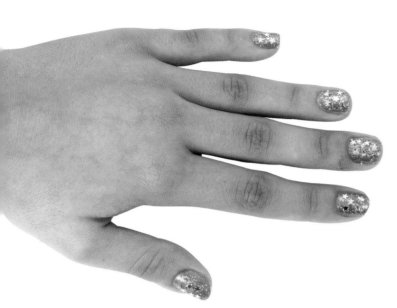

Here's what you do

1 Apply a base coat of blue polish. Let it dry.

2 Apply a coat of silver glitter polish.

3 While the glitter is still wet, dip the toothpick into clear polish and use it to pick up the stars. Press two or three stars to each nail. Then let it dry.

4 Paint two coats of clear polish over the stars.

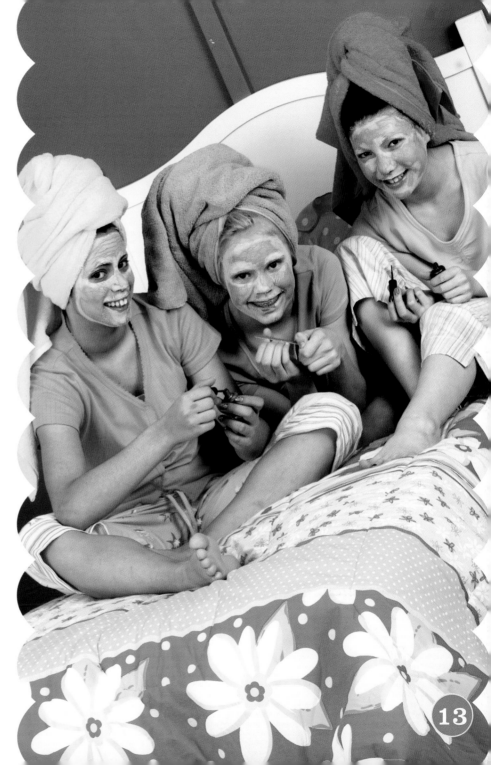

13

CHAPTER 5

Fabulous Flower Girl

Make your nails bloom with beauty.

Bring a whole new meaning to painting your nails. For this project, you'll use actual paintbrushes and **acrylic paint**. But don't worry. You don't have to be Van Gogh to paint a few little flowers.

Why paint instead of polish? The paint works better for small details. And yes, it comes off with the nail polish remover just like regular polish.

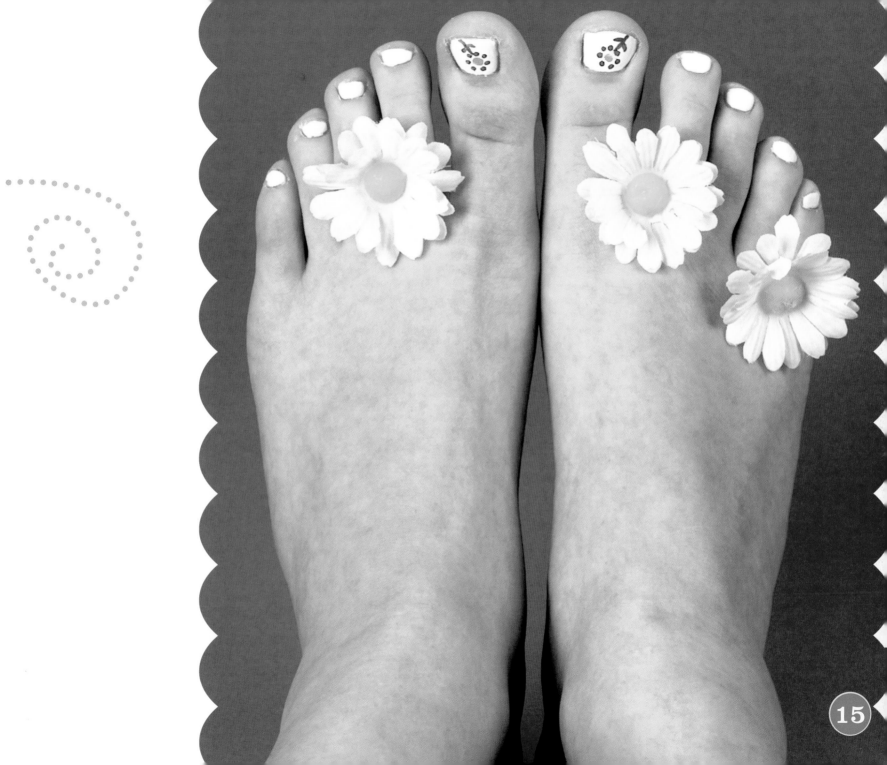

Here's what you need

* nail polish for base color(s)
* acrylic craft paints for flower designs
* small plate or dish
* cotton swabs
* small, natural hair paintbrushes
* clear nail polish

REMEMBER!

Safety Tip

Never use nail polish remover on broken skin or open sores. It can irritate the sore and cause further damage.

Here's what you do

1 Apply base color. Let it dry.

2 Put a small amount of craft paint onto a small plate or dish.

3 Use a cotton swab to make a round dot in the center of your nail. Then paint petals and stems with your paintbrushes.

4 When your flowers are finished, apply two coats of clear polish to help keep your blooms fresh.

Protect Your Paintbrushes

Very small, natural hair paintbrushes with pointed tips work best for nail art. But you need to take good care of them. Always clean your brushes in warm, soapy water. Rinse them in cold water. Then make sure the tips are nice and pointy. Let the brushes dry standing straight up in a jar, glass, or vase so the tips don't get smashed.

CHAPTER 6

Show Your Stripes

You can't go wrong with stripes.

What's the big deal with stripes? They're really just a bunch of straight lines next to each other. But when you play with the colors and the spaces between the lines, you make your own unique design. For this project, you'll be making stripes with nail foil. Think of them as your personal bar code.

Everything in Its Place

What do you do when you run out of room on your dresser to store all your nail polish and accessories? Try a cosmetic case. With all the little compartments, you'll be able to find a home for all your supplies.

Here's what you need

* nail foil
* scissors
* nail polish for base color
* clear nail polish
* toothpicks

Here's what you do

1 Cut the nail foil into small strips to fit diagonally across your nails. Don't worry too much about getting the length absolutely perfect. You can always trim them later with a small scissors.

2 Apply base color and let it dry.

3 Working on one nail at a time, apply a coat of clear polish.

4 While the clear coat is still wet, dip a toothpick into the bottle of clear polish and use it to pick up the foil strips. Place the strips diagonally on your nails. Let everything dry.

5 Apply two clear coats to seal.

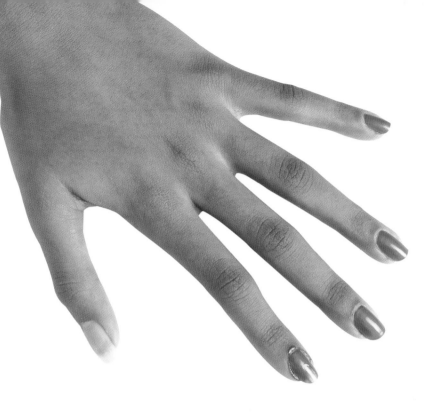

Sick of Smudges?
They happen to the best of us. But here's a tip: clean the smudges as soon as you see them. Take a cotton swab and wrap the end with tissue paper. Moisten it with polish remover, and use it like a pencil eraser to clean up.

CHAPTER 7

Emotions in Motion

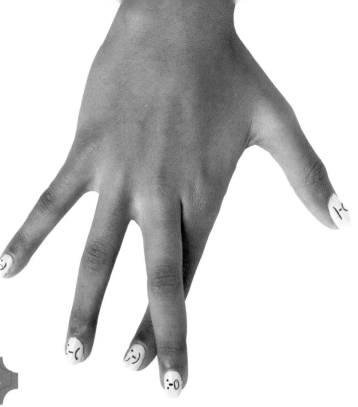

Keep your feelings at your fingertips.

If you're happy and you know it, your nails can really show it. Give people a clue by drawing **emoticons** on your nails. Are you joking or serious? Excited or bored? Happy or sad, flirty or funny, these quirky little e-mail symbols let everyone know your mood.

Get in Touch with Your Emoticons

:-) happy

:-(sad

;-) winking, joking

:-D laughing hard

I-O yawning, bored

:-P sticking out your tongue

Gooey to Glam

Is your fave polish too gooey to use? Don't trash it. Just add a few drops of polish remover to the bottle and shake it up. The polish might not be as shiny as it was before, so put an extra clear coat on top of it.

Here's what you do

1. Apply a base coat of yellow, white, or pink polish. Allow one hour or longer for the coats to completely dry. If you try using the markers before the base coat is dry, they won't work.

2. After the base coats are dry, use the markers to draw the emoticons on each nail.

3. Once the details of the emoticons are dry, apply one clear coat.

CHAPTER 8

Pretty Pop Princess

Wanna look like a glamorous pop diva?

Get out the nail stickers and rhinestones and jump onstage. This project is a great look for cheerleading, talent shows, or any other event that puts you in center stage.

Here's what you need

* nail polish for base color
* clear nail polish
* small nail stickers
* toothpicks
* small rhinestones

Party Like a Pop Star

Put a new spin on sleepover parties by renting a karaoke machine and singing your hearts out all night. Start the evening out by doing your hair, nails, and makeup like your favorite pop princesses. Then grab that microphone and sing like a superstar!

Here's what you do

1 Apply a base coat of polish. Repeat if necessary and let it dry.

2 Apply a coat of clear polish.

3 Working on one nail at a time, apply small dabs of clear nail polish along your nail tips.

4 Add stickers. Use a toothpick dipped in clear polish to pick the stickers up and place them on top of the clear polish.

5 Use the toothpicks to pick up the rhinestones and place them on the clear polish. Repeat with each nail.

6 Wait 15 minutes, and apply two clear coats to seal the rhinestones and stickers.

Soak It Off

Removing nail accessories like stickers and rhinestones isn't so hard. Soak a cotton ball in polish remover. Hold it on your nail for 3 minutes. Then press down and wipe. Accessories should loosen and pull off your nail. If it doesn't work the first time, don't panic. Just keep trying, and it will come off.

Fast Facts

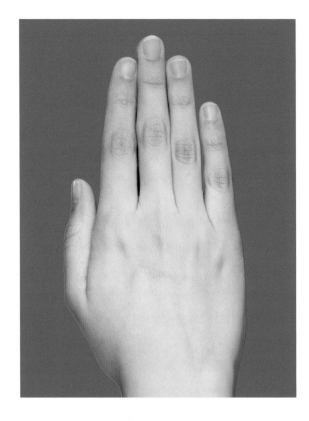

Nails Like an Egyptian

In ancient Egypt, some women dipped their fingernails in henna to color them. Henna is a red-brown dye made from the leaves of the henna plant. Today, people use it for hair dye and temporary tattoos. Some people still use it to color their toenails and fingernails, like the Egyptians did.

Did You Know?

Which of your fingernails grows fastest? If you're right-handed, it's the nail on your right middle finger. If you're left-handed, your left middle fingernail grows fastest. That's because the longer the finger, the faster the nail grows. And since you use your dominant hand more often, you put more pressure on the nails. The pressure encourages growth too.

Va-Va-Vroom!

Today, nail polish is made from the same kind of **enamel** as car paint. It is very hard and shiny and sticks well to flat surfaces, like fingernails. Only a chemical such as **acetone** or nail polish remover can remove it.

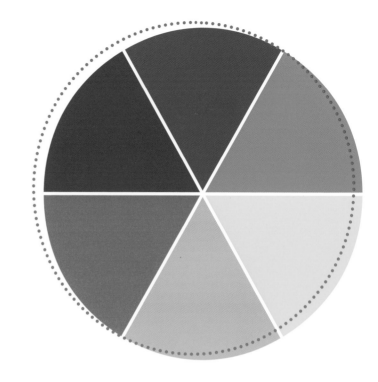

Color Wheel

Go beyond pink and red. These days you can find polish in every color of the color wheel. How do you choose? Remember that colors next to each other on the wheel work together in harmony. Colors opposite each other will have a stronger effect because they have more contrast.

Glossary

acetone (ASS-uh-tohn)—a toxic chemical used to remove hard enamels such as nail polish, car paints, and strong glues

acrylic paint (uh-KRIL-ik PAYNT)—a type of paint made from chemicals and often used for crafts

adhesive (ad-HEE-siv)—glue or other substance that makes things stick together

emoticon (ee-MOH-tuh-kahn)—a group of keyboard characters that stands for an emotion

enamel (i-NAM-uhl)—a type of paint that dries very hard and shiny

glamorous (GLAM-ur-uhss)—attractive and exciting

manicure (MAN-uh-kyur)—the cleaning, shaping, and polishing of the hands and fingernails

opaque (oh-PAKE)—difficult to see through

pedicure (PED-uh-kyur)—the cleaning, shaping, and polishing of the feet and toenails

rhinestone (RINE-stone)—a plastic jewel used in crafts and jewelry making

sealant (SEEL-uhnt)—a substance used to seal nail accessories to fingernails

Read More

Finger, Shari, and Susan Tumblety.
Fabulous Nails. Funtastic Kits. Lincolnwood,
Ill.: Publications International, 2000.

Haab, Sherri. *Nail Art.* Palo Alto, Calif.:
Klutz, 1997.

Williams, Julie. *Skin & Nails: Care
Tips for Girls.* Middleton, Wisc.: Pleasant
Company, 2003.

Internet Sites

FactHound offers a safe, fun way to find
Internet sites related to this book. All of
the sites on FactHound
have been researched
by our staff.

Here's how:

1. Visit *www.facthound.com*
2. Choose your grade level.
3. Type in this book ID **0736864741**
   for age-appropriate sites. You may also
   browse subjects by clicking on letters,
   or by clicking on pictures and words.
4. Click on the **Fetch It** button.

**FactHound will fetch the best sites
for you!**

About the Author

Thiranut Boonyadhistarn grew up in Tokyo, Bangkok, and Chicago. She learned various crafts in each country: origami in Japan, beading in Thailand, and paper crafts in America. The crafts she learned as a child have led to a lifelong love of the arts.

Boonyadhistarn has worked in film and TV production, graphic design, and book production. She also has written several kids' books on crafts. She lives in a tiny apartment in New York City, surrounded by boxes of glitter, rhinestones, and craft glue.

Index